# Rewriting The Rules of Success

## A Youth's Guide to Defying Societal Expectations and Achieving Greatness

DAMOR MCQUEEN

Printed in the United States of America.

**ISBN: 978-1-958443-92-7 (paperback)**

# *Dedication*

I dedicate this book to youth who are purpose-driven, passionate about the future and are on a mission to become the best version of themselves.

I also dedicate this book to the people whose shoulders I stand on—people like my father, grandmothers, other family members, mentors, coaches, and friends—people who are selfless and have contributed to my growth and development, no matter how small. I am because you are.

# Acknowledgments

Thank you to the global leaders—young and old—whose stories I used as examples of resilience. Your courage to live out loud has inspired us all.

Thanks be to God! He has been faithful all my life, and I would be nothing without His guiding hands.

# *Preface*

*"Our deepest fear is not that we are inadequate. Our deepest fear is that we are powerful beyond measure."*
*—Marianne Williamson*

One morning in 2017, while on my way to school, I had an epiphany that would forever change my life. As far back as I can remember, I struggled with acne. I hated having bumps suddenly pop up and having little control over this. Then, to complicate matters further, some individuals had the audacity to ask about the many bumps on my face. I was always a little discouraged by my ordeal until this one morning in 2017. This was the day I got some hope!

I still remember the bus I was on and where I was sitting when it all happened. I was overthinking about the bumps and a little worried when I heard clearly, *"The many bumps on your face represent the many lives you should impact."* Wow! What a powerful message! In no time, the Bumpy Purpose Campaign (now foundation) was formed by a few high school friends and me.

As you can tell, that day has forever changed my life and has led me to this moment. It has led me to you. God had better plans than my own disappointments and discouragement. So, as I write this book, I am reminded of why I am doing it. This is one of the many ways I intend to impact many lives. I am grateful that you are one of those people and you will share the book to impact even more lives. I believe this power to do big things and create impact is in all of us.

Have you ever felt like you were destined for more? Have you ever felt like your current state is not your final destination? I don't know about you, but I have. This drive has led me on a journey of self-discovery and has further led me to write this book. I am just a kid from rural Middleton in St. Thomas, Jamaica, fueled by my passion and purpose and on a mission to create positive global disruption. If you can identify with any of this, even if it is just a small piece of it, then this is the book for you. Read on as we rewrite the rules of success together.

Speaking of success, this was often a term I grew up hearing. In fact, the motto of my primary school was "Determination Leads To Success," and it was plastered on the front of the school building. I would often hear, "Work hard, and you will succeed." Without a doubt, these statements have some truths to them, but what exactly is success? Is it physical? Is it a feeling? A milestone? A new car, maybe? I think that all those could be successes because of a simple fact: success is subjective. In other words, what is success for you might not be a success for me, and vice versa.

As someone who has achieved a few milestones, it is safe to say I have had a few successes. From being a head boy in both primary and high school, student council president, youth mayor for my parish, having had a few TV interviews, to now studying at York University in Canada on a partial scholarship, these and other achievements might frame me as successful by the measurement of most people. Though these achievements are good, I believe the most rewarding part of all these successes is the fulfillment I get and the ability to positively impact other people's lives. That is success for me. That is why one of my favourite things to do while I was in Jamaica was to volunteer, especially at NexxStepp Lifelong Educational Services, a social enterprise founded by my mentor, Tishauna Mullings. Going in on a Saturday to read to the students or teach a new concept was the highlight of my day. I still believe I got the best sleep after a day of volunteering.

Another component of success for me is defying expectations. In other words, success is sweeter when I know I had to toil for it, for example, when I finally became student council president and had a seat on the school board. I say "finally" because I spent upwards of five years in the council before becoming president. I started out as a regular member; then I became assistant PRO, then PRO, vice president, and finally, president. You see, success takes time. The rewarding success, at least.

Success also requires starting small, even if it is just volunteering on a Saturday in your community or starting out as just a member of an organization. There is a scripture that sums this up really well. Zechariah 4:10a says, *"Do not despise these small beginnings, for the Lord rejoices to see the work begin." (NLT).*

With that being said, I wanted to talk to a generation of young people destined for greatness. I wanted to share a little of what I have learnt and some of the tools that continue to guide me on my journey to success and greatness. I wanted to break it down a little because sometimes we become so consumed by the grandness of things that we forget that big things start small.

There is a seed stage for every big tree, and there is a crushing stage for wine. Yes, my friend, there is a process. Don't get me wrong; I am not saying I am a pro and have all the solutions. All I am saying is that I have something to share. Let me share some of what I have learnt and am still learning. Let me share what my mentors and coaches have taught me. Let me share some of what life has taught me. Let us put things into perspective, and let us rewrite the rules of success together.

# How To Use This Book

In this book, I will share my life story and journey, and occasionally that of others, like some of the most famous people we love and admire, for example, Oprah Winfrey and Walt Disney, and history makers such as the Wright Brothers, and other movers and shakers. I will also share the stories of some young trailblazers such as Olivia Goodreau, Marley Dias, Greta Thunberg, and some of my friends like Rajae Lewis and Nebiyou Timotewos. And to put things into perspective, there are what I call "Power Steps" at the end of each chapter. These are at least three practical steps to help you take action on what you would have read in the chapter. I urge you to take these steps seriously, as they are important on your journey to success and greatness.

Finally, there is a theme song at the end of each chapter. Yes, you heard me right. A theme song! Some of the songs may or may not suit your taste, but that is not the point. I encourage you to listen to the words of the songs. Please listen to the song before moving on to the next chapter. There are occasional references to scriptures, thoughtfully woven in to complement some of my points without aiming to sway perspectives.

Also, it is okay to revisit the chapters and the power steps for refreshments and reminders. In fact, I suggest that you do so now and then, even after reading the entire book. After all, this is not a one-time fix. Remember, success is a journey.

Are you ready to have fun as we explore my rules for success? Let's go!

# Table of Contents

# Rule # 1

## Don't Run With The Herd

*"If you are always trying to be normal, you will never know how amazing you can be."*
*—Maya Angelou*

This quote by American poet and civil rights activist, Maya Angelou, sums up the cost of being normal and embracing the herd mentality; you lose your identity and authenticity. For clarity, according to the Merriam-Webster dictionary, herd mentality is the tendency of the people in a group to think and behave in ways that conform with others in the group rather than as individuals. In other words, you try to fit in just to be accepted. I was first introduced to this concept through Bishop TD Jakes' sermon, "Don't Run With The Herd," where he implored listeners not to conform or try to fit in. As you can imagine,

I was inspired by not fitting in, and being a little weird has always been my normal for as far back as I can remember.

I was born and raised in St. Thomas, Jamaica, and grew up in a small community called Middleton. While growing up, I was very involved in my school and community. I have no clear memory of my preschool years (basic school, as we say in Jamaica), but I remember my primary or elementary school years quite vividly. I went to Middleton Primary School, which was basically opposite my house. In fact, the community centre and playfield were also there. In primary school, I was one of the very few, if not the only male, to be as involved in school life, especially co-curricular activities. I was an all-rounder. I was a part of the school's spelling bee team, which saw me participating in the annual Gleaner's National Spelling Bee Competition for at least three years in a row. Though I never won at the parish level and moved on to the national finals, participating in the spelling bee was undoubtedly instrumental in giving me a firm academic foundation. Then there was the Little Genius Competition, which was perhaps in its first or second staging when I participated. This competition further grounded me and gave me the push I needed to eventually aspire for more. The Little Genius Competition is a character-building and critical-thinking competition for children at the primary school level. The competition was founded by Tishauna Mullings, who would later become a mentor and a significant part of my support system. You will hear more about my support system later on.

Then there was leadership. My primary school years also saw me becoming the head boy of the school and, later on, one of two valedictorians for the graduating class. However, it was my head boy role that gave me that very first taste of leadership. As head boy of the institution, I led a team of students who essentially oversaw the school compound. I remember being assigned a team of students to help me ensure that the school compound was clean and tidy and that things were generally orderly. This early taste of leadership was a crucial launching pad as it would be time for high school in a few years.

My high school years were equally rewarding. My admission to the prestigious Morant Bay High School came with much applause and excitement, as it was, and still is, one of the most sought-after high schools in the region and, arguably, Jamaica. High school was an opportunity for me to find myself and my voice.

On orientation day, I remember feeling friendless and scrambling to find new friends, as I was the only one from my primary school who was admitted to Morant Bay High School that year. Little did I know that in a few years, this would not even matter because I would see myself again holding some of the top leadership positions in the school and going up the ranks of leadership throughout my high school years, and even being a member of the school board while I was president of the student council. Now that I look back, I can see the naivety of the child-like mind. Little did I know that the best was yet to come!

I was introduced to and started in the student council from very early in high school. I was a student council member for five years straight before finally giving the role a break to take up the post of head boy. My student council years were my most rewarding though. I started out as just a regular member, eventually becoming an acting public relations officer (PRO) while in lower school, later the PRO, acted as vice-president on more than one occasion, then eventually held the top post as student council president. This new role saw me being appointed to the school board to represent the student population. With the prestige also came the urgent responsibility of defending and protecting the rights of students, and that I did.

My time as student council president saw my council hosting what we called the "School Fi Chat" town hall meeting, which was the first of its kind. The town hall saw students coming face-to-face with the student council and school leadership and voicing their concerns about issues affecting them. These town halls were a mastermind and, as a result, huge successes. Upcoming student council bodies would later replicate them. I also participated in the school pageant and was placed second, and I was also involved in clubs and societies.

High school presented many opportunities to run with the herd. For many, high school is where they fall victim to peer pressure. I have seen this first-hand during my time in student leadership. While in high school, I remember wearing loose-fitted khaki pants in an effort to abide by school rules and be a "model student." Big khaki pants were definitely not in style. "Tight pants" were the preferred choice for many, but that was not my style. Even then, I had to make a decision not to run with the herd. Remember, like me, you do not need to jump on every trend.

In addition to school leadership, there was also my community involvement. While head boy and towards the end of my high school years, I would later become Youth Mayor for my parish, St. Thomas. How this even happened is another story and certainly God's doing. You will hear more about this in the book.

My tenure as youth mayor was equally as rewarding. In the role, I represented hundreds of youth on a much bigger stage and at the parish and national levels. As youth mayor, I chaired a mock session of the municipal council, was invited to civic events, represented the actual mayor at a few of these events, and spoke in front of an audience of mayors and other leaders at the Youth Mayor's Forum and, later, in front of the Prime Minister of Jamaica, The Most Honourable Andrew Holness and a room of reporters. While youth mayor, I also appeared on television, telling a reporter of my plan to host a series of town hall meetings right across the parish in order for youths to voice their concerns and also speaking on the issue of unemployment, which, in my opinion, was a hindrance to the parish's development.

I know that all this might sound like all work and no play, but that is far from the truth. I did have fun too. I had a very

"Jamaican childhood." I played marbles participated in sports day, played football in the rain, climbed trees to pick mangoes, and swam in the river (which was my favorite thing to do when I visited my father), to name a few. Now that we have cleared that up, back to the point I was making earlier.

As you can see, each post, position, and action was a stepping stone to the next big thing, even if I didn't notice it at the time. There is therefore power in taking action and not running with the herd. Let's be honest: running with the herd is easy. It's human to want to fit in and find community. I am in no way saying that community is bad, but sometimes it can be, especially when it shields you from your identity and authenticity. For some reading this book, you struggle with your identity, which is okay. You won't have everything figured out all at once. Life is a journey, not a destination. So, be patient with yourself. There are, however, practical steps and adjustments you can make as you seek to embrace your own journey and identity. These will be explored at the end of the chapter.

This is not to say I haven't had my slip-ups. But I think I can partly credit growing up in the church to having this sense of direction. However, as I have grown, especially now in my 20s, embracing that uniqueness has become increasingly harder. I am being honest. There are so many distractions and the pressure to fit in and conform to the status quo. Sometimes, I do fall short. Nevertheless, I have to remind myself that my uniqueness is my superpower and that it is my uniqueness that has brought me this far. You see, it might be tempting to fit in, and sometimes we might even fall to the temptation, but it is never too late to rediscover your uniqueness. When you find it, nurture it because it is better to be an original rather than a copy. Embrace your uniqueness.

Your uniqueness might even isolate you and put you in the "weird" column. But with time, you will find your tribe because real knows real. So, don't be discouraged; it will all work out in the end.

Embracing my uniqueness has taken me places, but it also reminds me how far I can go. Remember, running with the herd is not an option. Is there any hype in being a member of a gang, a troublemaker, and a menace to society and to others? No, there isn't. There is simply no hype in running with the herd. Running with the herd could get you in jail or worse. On the contrary, there is hype in trodding your own path and motivating and uplifting others. This could get you in front of the prime minister and even turn you into the prime minister.

But being different will cost you something, whether that be your status in the group or being labeled as a nerd or even feminine (for the males). This can be hurtful. Trust me, I know. I have been there. I know what this isolation feels like, but looking back, it was worth it. The reward of staying different far outweighs trying to run with the herd.

Just look at Walt Disney, co-founder of The Walt Disney Company, who was fired from Kansas City in 1919 because, according to his editor, he "lacked imagination and had no good ideas." You see, sometimes rejection is simply redirection and a setup for even bigger things. Just imagine if Walt Disney had not been rejected. Perhaps the Disney Channel we love so much would not have existed today. Then, there were other successes, such as that of J.K. Rowling. Have you heard of Harry Potter? I'm pretty sure you have. Well, J.K. Rowling is the author of the Harry Potter series. Despite numerous rejections from publishers, Rowling persevered; the rest is history, as they say. There is power in persistence and staying hopeful, even after rejection. Don't lose hope because you could literally become the next big thing.

As I close this chapter, I want to encourage those who might actually be running with the herd. I want to say that it is never too late to change course and do the right thing. It is never too late to tread your own path on your journey to success and greatness. If you need help, find help. Refuse to stay stuck in a place that limits your growth and development. There are people, like myself, who are rooting for you. I am excited to see you win. You've got this!

## POWER STEPS

1. Firstly, get in touch with your passion. What is it that you really love doing? What brings you joy and, by doing it, could bring others joy? What value can you

add to society? This might require you to step away from the crowd for a moment and examine yourself. Take ten minutes to reflect on these questions. For me, I am now confident that my passion is youth development, and that passion has led me to write this book and, as a result, led me to you. I know it's perhaps a little weird to say my passion is youth development, as I am a youth myself, but it really is. Uplifting youth is what brings me joy. I am passionate about paving the way for generations to come, even if that is just through mentorship or volunteering in my community, which I have done for years. I would go home after a day of volunteering with children and youth and have the best sleep ever. That is how I know.

2. Secondly, stop running with the herd. You will have to make a decision here. I am not saying you should unfriend your friends, but maybe you should unfriend a few. I am joking (but kinda not). I would say approach this in phases. First, do an evaluation. Ask yourself, is this friendship bringing me value? Is this a good ROI (return on investment)? If the answer is no, you might need to start the process of disengagement. Notice I said might? This is because some friendships are probably worth saving, especially if that friend is someone you can convince to change course with you in the short term. If you think this person meets the criteria, then sit down and have a hard conversation. If they refuse to change,

then you need to change direction. That friend is probably not for you and for where you are going. It is a hard pill to swallow, but it is also the truth.

3. Lastly, pursue your passion and purpose. Remember I told you to identify your passion? Good! You remember! Now I want you to pursue it. I want you to take steps to actively perform it. If it is leadership, pursue it. If it is the performing arts, pursue it. If it is music, pursue it. Whatever it is, pursue it because this could be the gateway to your purpose. Your purpose is what you were placed on this earth to do, and your passion usually leads to your purpose.

**Theme Song: "I Was Here" (Beyonce)**

# Rule # 2

# Take Responsibility for Your Future

*"You can't escape the responsibility of tomorrow by evading it today."*
*—Abraham Lincoln*

In my second year of university, I enrolled in an International Politics course, which introduced me to a very eye-opening political theory: the Realism Theory. Just so you know, as I write this book, I am in my fourth year of university, majoring in Political Science. I am a big political enthusiast. For clarity, let us first define a theory. Simply put, a theory is basically an idea that intends to explain something or answer a question. The realist theory views the international system as a group of countries vying for power and domination, all with each having its own self-interest. This is why some realist theorists propose that it is the responsibility of individual countries to fend for and protect themselves in this international system. In other words, countries should not depend on or expect other countries to save them but should instead seek to save themselves. I mention realist political theory to articulate the title of this chapter. You, my friend, should take responsibility for your future.

On my very first flight in 2021, during the height of the COVID-19 pandemic, one of the instructions the flight attendant gave was how to utilize the oxygen mask during a potential emergency situation onboard. "In the event of an emergency," the flight attendant said, "ensure you have on your oxygen mask before you try to assist anyone else." Those words might sound selfish to some, but what is the point of saving others when you are also vulnerable and need saving yourself? We have to take responsibility for ourselves and our future.

The point that I am trying to make is that this life is a personal responsibility. You were the responsibility of your parents while in the womb, but as you grow older, you will have to take responsibility for your own future. No one is coming to save you. You will have to save yourself. Maybe you grew up in tough circumstances. Maybe you were verbally or physically abused, or maybe you were even neglected. Whatever the situation, the truth is that the power to change the course of your life lies within you.

Sometimes, we get caged by a victim's mentality. I get it; life definitely has its challenges. Some of us were not born into the best of situations, but regardless of this, you have a personal responsibility to create a better future for yourself and the generations to come. Let your story be one of triumph and resilience. Let history remember you as an overcomer. Rewrite your story if you must.

History is filled with people who rewrote their stories by taking personal responsibility. I will give you the life story of a few such individuals. Firstly, Oprah Winfrey, someone I admire a lot and is a role model to many around the world. Today, Oprah Winfrey is a well-known billionaire and former host of the Oprah Winfrey Show, which touched lives around the world, but there are a few things that came before this success and impact that many, including you, might not know about, so let me take you back.

Oprah Winfrey was born into poverty in rural Mississippi to a single mother. She was molested during her childhood and early teenage years and became pregnant at fourteen. The child died prematurely. Despite her rough upbringing, Winfrey went on to become the founder and CEO of Harpo Productions, the founder of The Oprah Magazine, and a renowned television host. She was also awarded the Presidential Medal of Freedom by President Barack Obama. She is also an actress who has received numerous awards, including honorary degrees, and is known for her philanthropic efforts around the world. Did I mention that she is a billionaire? The list continues.

The point though is that she saved herself. She took personal responsibility. She could have used the fact that she was born into poverty, was molested, and became pregnant at just fourteen years old as an excuse not to work hard and achieve success. But thankfully, she didn't. Life threw bricks at her, but she used them to build a stage for herself and others. What will you do with your bricks?

Then there are young people like Olivia Goodreau, who was bitten by a tick when she was six years old and, as a result, was diagnosed with chronic Lyme disease in addition to five other tick-borne diseases. This did not stop her. At age twelve, Olivia founded the LivLyme Foundation to provide assistance to children suffering from Lyme disease and help fund scientists conducting research surrounding Lyme and tick disease. Today, she is a well-known advocate for Lyme disease research and education and is the author of "But She Looks Fine: From Illness to Activism."

There is also my friend and brother, Nebiyou Timotewos, whom I met at York University. Nebiyou grew up in Ethiopia and would later move to Yemen, where he saw the destruction of war firsthand and grappled with the death of some of his closest friends and family. He and his family eventually moved to Canada, where they lived in a shelter for seven months. Today, at just twenty years old, Nebiyou is the founder of Brothers4Brothers, an organization aimed at creating a safe space for young men to uplift, inspire, and support each other. He also founded Communities Care, where he feeds the homeless and gives back to his community. Additionally, Nebiyou's name is synonymous with kindness as he is known for his "Kindness Tours," where he travels in and outside Canada, spreading kindness and uplifting others. He is an internationally recognized, award-winning youth and community leader. Nebiyou's story is one of resilience and should inspire us all to move forward despite life's challenges, and spread kindness to those we encounter. Let us be the light we want to see in the world.

It would be remiss of me not to mention here my own father, who is also the epitome of resilience. Just before my mother's burial, in fact, at an event celebrating her life, my father's hand was mutilated. But guess what? This did not stop him then and not even to this day. My father knew he had a child to care for despite his impediment. I was about three years old at the time. As I write this book, I am twenty-three years old. I have seen my father's resilience. From farming ground provisions to rearing chickens, cows, and goats to never missing an important milestone or achievement in my life, I have definitely seen resilience modeled before my eyes.

Like these amazing and resilient individuals, we should never allow our circumstances to define us, but we should instead find the power to rise above them. Thankfully, that power lies within all of us. The ball is in our court. I never allowed the death of my mother nor the disability of my father to be an excuse not to strive for excellence. In fact, it was these and other circumstances that have served as a motivation for me on my journey to greatness. It all comes down to perspective. If you see situations as obstacles, then you will become a victim. But if you see them as opportunities, then you will become a victor. To this day, I see these unfortunate situations as opportunities for me to progress, inspire, and uplift others. I am telling you that the power lies within you. You have the power to change the course of history.

However, you must first realize that no one is coming to save you. Take responsibility for your own future. Change starts with you.

## POWER STEPS

1. Firstly, take a few minutes of quiet time to answer this question: What has made you a victim? This is not for you to blame yourself or be hard on yourself. In fact, congrats for being brave enough to acknowledge potential shortcomings. After you have discovered those situations, then secondly:

2. Decide not to be a victim anymore. Create and repeat daily affirmations. After you have identified those issues, you will have to make a decision. Decide not to be held back by your past. Instead, decide to be a victor. Here is an example of an affirmation: *"I refuse to be a victim of my father being absent. I will instead be a victor and a great support system for my children in the future."*

3. Hold your head up high and work to change the narrative. Remember that it will be a work in progress. Things won't change overnight, so be patient with yourself and give yourself grace. You've got this!

**Theme Song: "Roar" (Katy Perry)**

# Rule # 3

# Get Yourself A Support System

*"No man is an island. No man stands alone."*
*—John Donne*

While in primary school, I was introduced to the solar system. I was taught that there were eight planets that revolve around the sun, each having its own orbit. The idea of a "system" is very important to understand as I explain the concept of a support system and why you need one on your journey to success.

The Merriam-Webster dictionary defines a system as *"a regularly interacting or interdependent group of items forming a unified whole."* In other words, a system has separate parts that function together to achieve a specific outcome. Let us now define "support." The Merriam-Webster dictionary defines it as *"to assist or help."* So we could then say that *"a support system is connected parts (in this case, people) working together to help you succeed."*

I have been using the term "support system" for many years now in reference to my family, mentors, coaches, and friends who provide guidance and support as I navigate life, my goals, dreams, and aspirations. Let me start off by telling you about my family and their role as part of my support system. Earlier I told you that my mother died when I was about three years old, and my father lost his hand and thus became disabled during this period. I guess you might be wondering how I survived because clearly, I did, right? Well, I grew up with my maternal grandmother, Donna Henry, who was a basic school teacher for twenty-nine years. I sometimes credit my academic success to this as I was going to school with my grandmother even before I was at the age to be an actual student. I lived with my grandmother for twenty years before leaving to study in Canada.

Then there is my father. He was knocked down but definitely not knocked out. My father has been a great source of strength and support all my life. He never once sat idly by, despite having a disability. In fact, I often say, *"to call my father disabled would be an insult."* My father is perhaps more abled than most people with both hands. From raising chickens, cows, goats, and farming, my father has never disappointed but has helped to support me financially and otherwise. He never made his disability an excuse to not be a father, and for that, I am forever grateful. Now that I am in

Canada, I speak with my father and grandmother almost every day; a testament to our bond and their impact on my life.

Then there are my aunts, uncles, grandaunts, and cousins, who are also a major part of my support system. I am forever thankful to them as well for their support and guidance over the years. I often say that my cousins supplemented my being an only child. Who needs siblings when you have cousins like mine on both sides of the family? Definitely not me. While I might be the sun with my gravitational pull that keeps everything in orbit in my metaphorical solar system, my family is like the moon. They help in creating stability and being a source of light in the darkest of times.

There were, and still are, those people who are not biologically my family but are family. Tishauna Mullings, an early mentor, has been a key part of my success over the years. I first met Tishauna in primary school when I participated in her company's Little Genius Competition, a critical thinking and character-building competition for children. I later reconnected with Tishauna while in high school. Fate would have it that she was hosting an impromptu public speaking competition at my school for career day when my friend, Shantae, came running and hurriedly grabbed me to participate. I did and won. That was how we reconnected. From advice on life and leadership to preparation for television interviews and hosting duties, Tishauna remains a crucial part of my journey. There are so many other people, like Tishauna, that I would consider mentors and who are also an important part of my journey—a big thank you to every one of them.

Then there are also teachers like Mrs. Marsha Ford-Bryan, who was an important part of not only my academic journey but also my overall personal development. Mrs. Ford-Bryan is one of those teachers who encourages you to participate in the high school pageant because she sees your potential, even if you don't. I was placed second in the pageant but won the hearts of many on the night. She was also the year supervisor for my cohort. She had us learn the qualities of the eagle and had us chanting *"We are eagles soaring high"* during morning devotion. I also worked with her to develop arguably one of the most unique and fun valedictory addresses ever. To this day, people message me asking about the introduction to follow suit for their class projects or other valedictory addresses. Thankfully, Mrs. Ford-Bryan is one of many such educators. There are so many educators who have had a significant impact on my growth and development throughout my life, and I am forever grateful. Mentors like Tishauna Mullings and Mrs. Ford-Bryan are like the asteroid belt in my solar system. They help to influence my evolution.

It would be remiss of me not to also mention my coaches, who remain instrumental on my journey. Crystal Daye, who, through her book-coaching company, has provided guidance as I write this book. Odetta Rockhead-Kerr, who, through her coaching as it relates to my financial future and impact, helped nurture my vision to write this book. There are two important takeaways here. Firstly, your support system will expand as you grow and will also expand your horizon, so be open to newness. You also need to be cautious because there are people who will only support the successful version of you and completely neglect the processing. Secondly, life is a journey, and people will come and go. As is often said, people come into our lives for seasons. So, when people do leave, find the courage to move forward. You are still awesome, and you have a great journey ahead of you, regardless of who might have left or who will eventually leave. Always remember that God will send others to help you along your journey. The best is still yet to come. If my mentors are the asteroid belt in my solar system, then my coaches are the kuiper belt. They serve as a reservoir for my replenishment and upliftment.

My friends have also been a huge part of my support system. I will mention just a few of them here. My friend, Keyshawn, who I met at a leadership conference in 2016, remains a source of inspiration and upliftment. Then there is another friend with a similar name, Keishane, who I met in high school while in student leadership and who was from another school. This is the friend I called one night when I felt like I was having an anxiety attack as a result of feeling stressed while having a paper to submit. At the time, my friend was in university studying counseling and was able to provide expert support. Thankfully, I was able to calm myself down and submit my assignment.

I met my friend, Chevelle, in church. She has been a champion of my successes over the years. Our friendship throughout the years involved us speaking positively over each other's life. I am glad to now see many of those positive words and affirmations coming to life.

Then there is Jazzele, a long-time high school classmate who has been a major supporter over the years, usually having a leadership role in and supporting all my initiatives. A part of my reason for mentioning these different individuals is to show how different all our friendships can be. I have a different relationship with all my friends, and each friend serves a different purpose at times. Friendships, like all other relationships, should also be about reciprocity. The least you can do is to check in on your friends now and then. Never just assume that they are okay. You did not think I forgot the planets, did you? My friends are the planets in my solar system. Each planet contributes to the diversity of the solar system and plays a key role in stabilizing the system. My friends bring that stability and diversity.

There are also friendships that are fairly new. Another lesson is to be open to friendships. I know that in a world that now normalizes being alone and cutting people off, this can be hard. However, in the same way someone could bring you down, they could also lift you up. It is all about perspective. Don't let one or a few bad experiences lock you in a box and make you believe that everyone is the same.

Let me also pause to recognize some of those who have passed on but were key to my support system. My paternal grandmother, Verleta Chambers, my church mother, Mother Brown, and an elderly lady I randomly met and who became a huge part of my support system, Miss Pet. It is important to note that I have only mentioned just a few of the people who have supported me along the way. After all, I wouldn't be able to mention everyone. So, if you have contributed to my successes so far, in any way, no matter how small, thank you. Your support has led me to this moment. God, who is the gravity in my solar system, was intentional about placing you in my life, and I am grateful for that.

Get yourself a support system. If you already have one, consider the role that each individual plays in your life. Are they the moon, the asteroid belt, kuiper belt, or the planets? Life can be tough at times, and you will need support along the way. Again, don't let a few bad apples make you believe that everyone is bad. I am not telling you to go dump all your secrets on someone you consider your friend. Remember, friendships take time and there are different levels to friendships. It is possible to be closer to one friend than another. Spend time to nurture your friendships.

Also, seek out mentors and coaches because you will also need them. Your mentors get into rooms that you don't and, as a result, can direct you to opportunities. Finally, lean into your family. I know what you are thinking. You are probably saying something like, "I don't even trust my family," or "Family can be the worst," and I get you, but I am sure they are not all bad. Again, don't let a few bad apples make you think that all the apples are bad.

Sadly, life can be so unpredictable. One day people are here, and the next day they are gone, so check in and stay connected. Relationships take time. Be intentional about building your support system. You need people in your life who see your potential and who help to nurture it. And as you build your support system, remember that people will come and go (kinda like Pluto in the solar system). But this is a part of the journey. Embrace the journey.

## POWER STEPS

1. Be intentional about forming new connections. Remember, forming new connections is not bad. The right support system can add value to your life. Being intentional about forming connections could be as simple as sending someone a private message over zoom after being intrigued by what they had to say on the call or attending events and connecting with other attendees via social media.

2. Maintain these connections (check in). Yes, you also need to be intentional about maintaining these connections. Check in with these individuals at least twice per year. Like their posts on social media. Stay relevant and be deliberate about maintaining the connections you have formed.

3. See it as an investment in your future. Sometimes adding people to your support system might come with a financial commitment, especially if the individual you are seeking to connect with is a coach. If this is the case, I urge you to view this as an investment in yourself. Think about the value you can potentially get from connecting with that individual via their coaching services. You would buy the latest shoes, so why not buy into your future self? Think about that.

**Theme Song: "We're All In This Together" (High School Musical and Walt Disney)**

# Rule # 4

## Invest In Your Future Today

*"The future belongs to those who prepare for it today."*
*—Malcolm X*

I was first introduced to the concept of "investing" in one of my business-related classes taught by one of my high school teachers. Though she did not stay on the topic for too long, sitting at the front of the class, the concept sounded quite interesting. *"You get to own a small piece of the company,"* she said as she went on to the next bullet point. It was, however, not until I came to Canada that I really understood what my teacher was saying as my interest in finance and money management grew. I am also learning that investing doesn't have to be monetary. In fact, one can invest in oneself and their future in a myriad of ways.

In this chapter, I will touch on five such ways of investing in oneself: physically, intellectually, spiritually, socially, and financially.

Physical investment in your youth is crucial. Though sometimes neglected because of our "youthfulness," our physical health is very important and should be given priority. Remember, we won't be young forever. Additionally, there are illnesses such as diabetes and heart conditions that have become increasingly common among young people. So, start by looking at what is going into your body. Ask yourself, *"Is this a good investment in my physical health?"* Is there a positive return on investment? If not, then you have your answer. Also, get active. For many people like me, that could involve going to the gym for a few days of the week. If this is new for you, you could start off with just one day, then gradually increase the number of days. You could even go for thirty minutes per day and gradually increase the amount of time you spend in the gym. For me, I started off with at least an hour. Now, after consistently going for over a year, that hour has increased to one hour and fifteen minutes up to one hour and thirty minutes, depending on the sets of workouts I am doing for the day. The point, however, is that you should get started, no matter how small.

Good habits, like bad ones, compound. For some people, physical activities are done at home. That was also me during the pandemic. I had time on my hands, so I started working out from home. I downloaded a workout app that tracked my progress, and during that period of working out, I saw results. Whatever your preference, get started.

I also want to mention stress here because it affects youth too. I grew up hearing adults talk about high and low blood pressure, but at the time, this all seemed so foreign for a mere teen, until one day it wasn't. I remember the day quite vividly. I was still in Jamaica and in high school. I left the house to collect a package in the town when suddenly everything around me started to spin and I was dizzy. Thankfully, I was able to hold on to a structure and beckoned to a random lady on the street who braced me up and brought me to a family friend who was selling in the nearby arcade, upon my request. Soon after, I called my aunt, Kaysha, and in a short time, my father came by to carry me to the doctor. At the doctor, I learnt that my blood pressure was too high for my age, and what I experienced was called vertigo. It is basically a condition where you have the false sensation that your environment is spinning or that you are off-balance. As you can see from my own experience, even youth can become stressed. I was burdening myself with a lot and it all came tumbling down.

Sometimes life can be so overwhelming, but at least try not to make the burdens and disappointments that come with life weigh you down. Protect your mental health at all costs. Take a break from social media, for example, if that becomes necessary for you. Prioritize "me time." Take some time to meditate even. Put on some music, close your eyes, and relax. Try to tune out the noise. Also, remember that support is available through your schools, universities, community groups, and even your support system. Ask for help. You do not have to carry the burdens of life alone. Invest in your future physical health today.

Also, invest in yourself intellectually. Expand your knowledge. Learn as much as you can as often as you can. Outside of my political science major, I have developed a love for finance. As a result, I consume a lot of investment and personal finance content through YouTube, podcasts, and audiobooks, and I even try to get into rooms and spaces where those topics are being discussed. When I am at the gym, I listen to the Ramsey Show, a financial podcast in the US, when I am not listening to music. During my over one-hour commute to campus, I listen to audiobooks, ranging from finance to personal development. I practically live on YouTube. I am subscribed to numerous channels aimed at personal development, finance, and politics, and I follow many more on social media. Create an environment for learning. Expand your knowledge and expand your world.

Then there is spiritual investment. I know this section might not be for everyone but I invest in my relationship with God. I believe that all my successes are a result of God and His goodness towards me. Simply put, I am nothing without God.

I grew up in the church and, over the years, I have learnt the importance of having a personal relationship with God. Emphasis on the words "personal" and "relationship." Never neglect fostering that intimacy with God. This could involve reading the Bible daily, even if it is just a verse for the day, praying, and reflecting on God's goodness. To each their own, but I have found that God is the source of my successes and my life, so I need to stay connected to the source.

Socially, you need to invest in solid relationships. One of the ways in which I have built solid relationships over the years is via direct messaging via Zoom, believe it or not. I would attend events and sessions hosted over zoom, listen to someone speak or introduce themself in the chat, and get really inspired. I would then send them a direct message and ask if they are interested in connecting. The rest, as they say, is history. That was exactly how I met my friend, Jamila, who also went to York University, was from Jamaica, and was on the same scholarship as me. She was doing the same major as I was. What a coincidence! We connected over zoom and arranged a meet-up on campus. She became a really good friend.

I have also connected with people all over the world who I have never met in-person but are also a part of my network today. Then there are the in-person connections where I attend an event, randomly meet someone I am fond of, and then exchange numbers or connect via LinkedIn. These connections are important because you never know what might come from them. Don't be afraid of networking and forming new connections. But also be discerning of the connections you make, as some people might have ulterior motives.

Another aspect of social investment is building social skills, such as communication skills. A good way to work on this skill is through a part-time job. All my part-time jobs have taught me valuable social skills—whether that was working as a sales associate at the mall, doing door-to-door marketing, or being a student mentor on campus.

Lastly, you need to invest in your future self financially, and this is one of my favourite. Let me, however, start off by saying that I am not a financial advisor, so what I say here is not financial advice. One of the major lessons I have learned so far is the importance of starting early on your investing journey and that investing does not have to be complicated. There are several financial investment options, including, but not limited to, stocks, bonds, index funds, and real estate. With that being said, I would suggest that you speak with a financial advisor and do additional research if you are interested in the subject. As they say, sometimes you will have to spend money to make money, and this is important to remember when it comes to financial investment. Sometimes, you might even have to spend money to acquire knowledge and make more money. For example, I once attended a paid virtual investment conference where real estate investing was being taught. It was just for one day and for a few hours, but I was inspired, and my knowledge expanded. I left the conference more informed and equipped with knowledge that could get me closer to my goal of becoming a millionaire. Consider a financial investment as making a financial deposit in your future self. It is a proven fact that financial investment is key to wealth creation.

## POWER STEPS

1. Start by doing your research. Some of these areas might require more extensive research than others. Financial investing, for example, might require more in-depth research.

2. Get connected. If you are into audiobooks, then you should probably get an audiobook subscription. Whatever the subject, also consider getting connected on YouTube by subscribing to the channels you are interested in. Thankfully, content surrounding all five areas can be found on YouTube.

3. Being connected could also mean forming connections in the areas you want to invest in. For example, connect with a friend and workout together. Also, connect with an actual financial advisor re financial investment.

**Theme Song: "My Day" (Tarrus Riley)**

# Rule # 5

# Date Yourself

*"The better you know yourself, the better your relationship with the rest of the world."*
*—Toni Collette*

In your quest for connections, whether that be romantic or otherwise, it is important that you not neglect connecting with yourself. I call this "dating yourself." In other words, before you try to get to know someone else, first get to know yourself. When you are in tune with yourself, you become a force to be reckoned with. Not only do you become less easy to manipulate, but this also builds confidence in one's self. Knowing one's self will also limit negative encounters with others because you then know when to shut up or step aside when offended, for example, before lashing out. I try my best to manage my facial expressions because I might not always say how I feel, but my facial expressions will.

Do you know your likes, dislikes, pet peeves, or what brings you joy? If not, that is okay, but this could be because you haven't really dated yourself. Your youth is an especially important time for you to do just this. Try new things, meet new people, and become exposed to the world, but also know your limits. I am not saying you should go skydiving if that is not your thing. I am not saying you should go clubbing if that is not your thing or is not in line with your own values.

In my second year of university, a classmate and his brother, after class, decided to take a smoke break and asked if I wanted to join them. I politely declined because that just wasn't my thing. I share this specific story because I want you to know that as you become more exposed to the world, you will come across people with different values and beliefs, and that is okay. My classmate wasn't a bad person because he was smoking. He simply had different values than I had, and that is just a part of life. When and if you do decide to travel or get an opportunity to do so, you will quickly notice that there is an entire world besides your world. There are different peoples, cultures, beliefs, and values, and you will have to coexist without giving up who you are. This is why you must know who you are. This is why you should date yourself.

In my first year of university, I enrolled in a course called "Justice for Children." On one particular day, we were discussing racial criminalization and the mass incarceration of young black men. This discussion made me extremely uncomfortable. I was one of maybe two or three black students in the class that day and was probably the only male. To complicate things, I felt as though everyone was looking at me, even if they weren't. Did I also mention that I was sitting at the front? The point though is that that moment was teaching me about myself.

On the bus ride home, I started to analyze the entire situation. What made me so uncomfortable to the point that I couldn't even speak? What was I to learn from this encounter about myself? These were some of the questions I asked myself. Upon reflection, I think the lesson I learnt about myself that day was that I am sensitive to the plight of my race, likely because, as a student of history, I am very familiar with our history of oppression. Looking back, I also realized that grappling with issues of racism and racial identity was never my lived experience, especially growing up in a country like Jamaica with a largely black population. In Jamaica, the issue would be colourism and not so much racism. That uncomfortable moment in class helped me realize all this.

Now, let us talk a little about love and romance. Humans are affectionate beings, so love and romance are a major part of our existence, but trying to get to know someone else when you don't even know anything about yourself is dangerous and potentially destructive. At least get to know your likes and dislikes. That way you can spot red flags before committing to a relationship. I am definitely not a relationship pro, but I think many relationships fail because people don't even know themselves, and they are trying to get to know someone else. Date yourself first.

I am not saying you will know yourself all at once or in an instant. After all, we humans are also very complex beings. I know this for a fact. For example, I like going out, but I also don't like going out (sometimes). Yes, even I am complex. The point is that I am still learning about myself, and you should too. The practical steps below will help you do this.

Spending time to date yourself will only help you get in touch with yourself and also help you love yourself. Get to know the good and bad because both will help to shape you and help you on your journey to success and greatness. Embrace you in your entirety. I talk extensively about this in rule 11.

## POWER STEPS

1. Reflect (moments of reflection). Sit still in the mornings or whenever works for you and reflect on your life, likes and dislikes and document them as you go along.

2. Literally go on dates with yourself. Yes, I mean it. This could include going to the movies or taking a walk, among other things. As you are out with yourself, take time to reflect and examine yourself. Listen to yourself the same way you would listen to someone else on a date.

3. Ask friends and families about traits they see in you. Have they noticed things you notice about yourself or don't? This is an opportunity to adjust what needs adjusting and to perhaps lean into what is working.

**Theme Song: "Unstoppable" (Sia)**

# Rule # 6

## Be A Sponge

*"Opportunities are like sunrises. If you wait too long, you miss them."*
*—William Arthur Ward*

When I was just about to begin studying at York University, I received one of the most inspiring and thought-provoking pieces of advice ever from someone on Instagram. The person simply said, *"Be a sponge."* Yes, that is the inspiring and thought-provoking advice. By that, the person meant that I should seize opportunities in university. Had they just said, *"Seize opportunities,"* it would not have had the powerful effect it had on me then and even to this day, so much so that when I sit on panels or speak to an audience, I usually tell them about that amazing advice I got some years ago.

If I am being honest, the idea of seizing opportunities was nothing new to me. In fact, the motto of my former high school, Morant Bay High School, is “Carpe Diem,” which is Latin for “Seize The Opportunity.” For students at the institution and past students like myself, that motto remains an important part of our development and lives. It was not until high school that I became strategic about seizing opportunities. Yes, I said strategic. More on that soon. Now that I reflect, during primary school, I really did not see opportunities such as student leadership as important in my overall development and, thus, a strategy for success. It was not until high school that I saw the immense benefits.

As you know by now, I was very involved in high school and seized many leadership opportunities. Again, this is partly because I saw the value in doing so and the long-term impact. Not only did my leadership roles in and out of high school help in my overall personal development, but they positioned me as a leader and came with some level of responsibility and even notoriety. As I mentioned earlier, in high school, I was a student councilor for five years before joining the prefect body as head boy of the institution. I understood the roles of both the student council and prefect body and the level of power and responsibilities that were found within each. You see, the prefect body is mainly for maintaining order in the institution while working hand-in-hand with the administration of the school. I must say that the prefect body has a level of prestige and notoriety but not so much the student council body. This is what I have noticed at least.

I love the prefect body, but if one truly knew the power that lies within the student council, one might be more inclined to learn more about and join the council. What many might not know is that the parliament of Jamaica, through the Education Act of 1980, gives the student council body, through its president, certain powers. Not only is the student council and its executive one of the chief defenders of students, but the council also has a seat on the school board. Yes, you heard me right. An act of parliament provides a seat at the table where the student council president gets to voice his or her concerns on issues affecting the student body and vote on future plans of the institution. I know what you are thinking, and the answer is "no." The prefect body does not have a seat on the school board. Nevertheless, both student bodies have their merits, serve very important roles, and help foster leadership. You can't go wrong being a part of either. So, to my point, leadership opportunities became effective for personal development and provided an opportunity to effect real change.

Then there was my role as youth mayor for my parish, St. Thomas, which came about very impromptu. For clarity, the youth council is a replica of the local or municipal government. So, in the same way you would have a mayor, elected councilors, and other representatives, students who are members of the youth council would take on those roles (youth mayor, for example) during their one-year tenure. The youth council is then given funds by the government to carry out projects and perform a mock session of the council. The youth mayor gets to represent his or her parish at the national level, meets with the prime minister for a courtesy call, and even gets to carry out some civic duties. Prior to assuming this role, I was part of the youth council perhaps two years before, but I was the junior CEO at that time. Fast forward to two years later, I accompanied the cohort of students who were to participate in the council for that year, along with the teacher in charge. However, I did not intend to participate. I helped the students with speeches and gave them a little pep talk. After they delivered their speeches, it was time to contend for the role of youth mayor. While sitting there, I thought, *"Why not contend for the role of youth mayor since I'm already here?"* Without prior preparation, I did just that, and that same day, I became youth mayor. This is what you call seizing opportunities.

I must say though that opportunities are not always in arm's reach, so sometimes you will have to go looking for opportunities. You won't always get the opportunities you go after, but at least you tried. When I worked in door-to-door marketing, I was taught that "NO" simply means "Next Opportunity." So, when I would knock on a door and get rejected, I reminded myself that it was not rejection but merely a set up for the next opportunity. I was always hopeful that the next door could be a "YES." This is the kind of mindset that you should develop because things will not always work in your favour. You will have to be resilient.

Another aspect of seizing opportunities that I want you to consider is seizing the opportunities your parents and even grandparents never had. I once had a conversation with my father. I asked him what he wanted to become when he was younger. I was surprised to hear that he did not know because, as a child, that was not even on his mind at the time. He was too busy focusing on survival. This conversation with my father was such a huge eye-opener. I am living in an opportunity that my parents never had. I am in university studying and have the opportunity to dream big. In fact, many of us are living in opportunities that our parents and grandparents never had. Some of them grew up in a time when they were faced with so many challenges that impeded their progress. I urge you to remember this as you seize opportunities. I urge you not to take the opportunities you have for granted.

As I write this book, I also sit on a Caribbean-affiliated scholarship committee in Canada as a student after being recruited to join, having received a bursary from the organization in my first or second year of university. Also, as I write this book, I am still in a joyous mode, having been invited to be the student speaker at the 2024 President's Reception for international students at my university. I remember attending this event in the past and being inspired, standing in the audience and taking in the spectacle. So, to have been asked to be the 2024 student speaker, I had to seize this once-in-a-lifetime opportunity. Sometimes opportunities will come running after you, especially when you position yourself for them. Say yes to opportunities until you can say no to opportunities. Try to get into as many rooms as possible. Expand your knowledge. Be exposed. Learn and grow. Get your feet wet. Be a sponge!

## POWER STEPS

1. Firstly, figure out what opportunities you are interested in. Are you a student and interested in student leadership opportunities? Are you an upcoming speaker or community leader? Decide on your interests. In other words, know what opportunities you are looking for because if you don't, you'll miss them.

2. Connect to those sources. Get in those spaces where the opportunities are. If you are an upcoming speaker, then connect with other speakers. Follow them on social media. Sign up to their email lists. If you are a student interested in leadership, connect with more senior student leaders.

3. Lastly, go searching for opportunities. Opportunities might not find you, so you might have to go find them. So, do not be complacent.

**Theme Song: "One Moment In Time" (Whitney Houston)**

# Rule # 7

## Be Your Own CEO

*"Do not speak bad of yourself. For the warrior within hears your words and is lessened by them."*
*—Unknown*

Everyone wants to be a CEO, right? Don't you? I'm going to assume the answer is yes. For the record, however, CEO here does not mean what you think it does, but you are pretty close. It is not Chief Executive Officer but instead Chief Encouragement Officer. Yes, I said what I said. You will have to become your own CEO and become good at it too. In a world with many ups and downs, there are many moments when we have to encourage and uplift ourselves. I am not opposed to motivational speakers on social media or even your family providing motivation but, trust me, there are times when you have to take on that role. So, get in the habit of motivating and uplifting yourself.

For me, I call them my "mirror moments." Sometimes I start to overthink, fear, worry, and doubt and quickly have to find myself a mirror. This is where the magic happens. *"Do you know who you are?"* I would say sometimes. *"You are Damor McQueen, and God did not bring you this far to leave you. In fact, the best is yet to come."* Yeah, I know. To some, this might sound crazy, but this is better than looking down on yourself. Sometimes the fighter in you just needs to know that they are still a fighter and that better days are ahead despite present challenges. After all, you have lived your life, and I am sure you have faced at least one challenge that felt overwhelming at the moment, but eventually, you overcame. Haven't you? I am sure you can at least think of one thing. Maybe it was just exam season for you. For some, it might be public speaking. For others, it might be the death of a family member which you haven't fully healed from, but you can admit that you are coping better than before. Whatever the case, you have made progress, and that is commendable.

The fact is, life will challenge you, and you will have to fight back. The only other option is to rollover and give up. That is not a viable alternative. Get your fight on! Making a decision to fortify your mind and fight back continuously will no doubt build your resilience over time and even position you as an overcomer. Whenever you face challenges and overcome them, you gain credibility. You are now in a position to tell others that things will be okay simply because you have experience. Or, as my grandmother would put it, *"Don't tell me about my toothache when you've never had a toothache."*

You see, no matter how great or powerful we are, we will sometimes have doubts and fears. After all, we are human. Whether you are thinking about starting a new business, going back to school, taking on a leadership role, or even doing something new, there will sometimes be fears and doubts. Former First Lady Michelle Obama, in her book, 'The Light We Carry,' calls this the *fearful mind.* She tells the story of her husband, Former President Obama, coming to her with his decision to run for president of the United States, but only if she agreed to it. She admits that she had fears but, thankfully, she did not give in to those fears. This could have quite literally changed the course of history. Her husband would not have become the first black president of the United States and her a phenomenal first lady.

Fear can cripple us if we allow it to thrive. So, do not allow it to thrive. As soon as it starts coming at you, shut it down. Remind yourself how great you are and of the challenges you have already overcome. Be mindful of how you speak to yourself because you will have to live with yourself.

I have spoken on many stages, including live television interviews, as I have mentioned before, and I can tell you for a fact that even the greatest speakers will have a little fear now and then. I still get a little nervous before I go on stage, but I find that two things help me calm and build my confidence. Firstly, those positive self-talks. I remind myself that I have done this before and that God is with me as He has always been. Secondly, I visualize the end result. After all, I would just be speaking for a few minutes and, in no time, those few minutes will end and I feel relieved and proud that I had the courage to do what I just did. I did not allow fear to cripple me, so I won. Feel the fear and do it anyway. That is how you grow and become better at your craft.

Greatness is on the other side of fear. Speak positively to the warrior in you. Be your own CEO.

## POWER STEPS

1. Take some time to document at least five positive attributes you possess and at least five victories you have had, no matter how small or insignificant you think they are. I want you to reflect on these and even memorize them.

2. Use these positive attributes and personal victories to develop positive self-talk. Have your **"mirror moments"** as often as possible. I suggest every day so it becomes a routine. This doesn't have to last for twenty minutes. At least look at yourself in the mirror and say, *"You are so beautiful, and great things are ahead for you."* When habits like this compound, they help position you for success.

3. Surround yourself with positivity. Be deliberate about this. Tailor your environment. Follow a few people you admire on social media, listen to positive songs like the ones found at the end of each chapter, and listen to motivational videos on YouTube. You definitely can't control everything or people's negativity, but you do have control over some things.

**Theme Song: "Encourage Yourself" (Donald Lawrence and The Tri-City Singers)**

# Rule # 8

## The Sky Is Not The Limit

*"There are no limits on what you can achieve with your life, except the limits you accept in your mind."*
*—Brian Tracy*

It is a century-old saying—and I hate to disappoint and mess with your belief—but the sky is really not the limit. Before you come for me, my father has my back because he also believes this and reminds me often. The truth is that there are no limits, unless you create them, of course. So, make a decision not to. Isn't it ironic that in our quest to say there are no limits, we are actually saying there is a limit, in this case, the sky? That statement in itself is therefore limiting. Furthermore, as a Christian, it is my belief that there is a destination beyond the sky. So, again, the sky is not the limit.

Like this quote, limiting beliefs can be subtle. They hang around even without us noticing. We recite them and they become facts to us. *"I'm not a speaker. I'm not eloquent enough. I can't do this. I can't do that."* This kind of belief system can be crippling. The Bible reminds us that *"death and life are in the power of the tongue." (Proverbs 18:21a - KJV).* As we constantly remind ourselves of what we can't do and recite the negative, it takes life, whether we notice it or not. This therefore requires a change in vocabulary. I suggest adding the word "yet" instead. For example, say *"I'm not a good public speaker yet."* By just adding this three-letter word, you have changed the entire meaning. "Yet" signals that it is achievable and gives you room to pursue it. It also speaks to the future possibilities. One of my favourite is *"I'm not a millionaire yet."* It is not so much if I will become a millionaire, but when. My mindset is preparing me for the millions.

You may or may not be familiar with the Wright brothers, but I am sure you are familiar with their invention. The Wright brothers, Orville and Wilbur Wright, are credited for inventing the airplane. For them, the sky was literally not a limit. Though this was never done before, they envisioned it and worked at making it a reality. I can only imagine how weird and even stupid they might have seemed to the people of their time. Nevertheless, they pushed beyond doubts and limitations and are known today and credited with inventing one of the most useful inventions, proving that there are literally no limits, not even the sky.

Then there is the amazing William Kamkwamba, who is known by some as "The Boy Who Harnessed the Wind." Those words might sound familiar because they are both the title of a book and a movie on the life of William Kamkwamba. So, who is he? He is a Malawian inventor and author who, at the age of fourteen and before his notoriety, built a windmill out of spare parts and scraps that generated electricity for his village. I love this story because for William Kamkwamba, there were no limits. Not even poverty could stop him.

It is also important that you remain focused, especially when you are doing what has not been done before, because, in the pursuit of your dreams and goals, you will have to fight off your own limiting beliefs and those of others. Do not let others project their own fears and doubts onto you and your big dreams. Sadly, these individuals will sometimes include family and loved ones. Sometimes, they are not deliberately trying to do so, but their worldview and exposure are sometimes just limited.

When I first travelled in 2021 to begin school in Canada, one of the things I often said, and still hope for everyone, especially young people, is for them to get an opportunity to travel internationally, even if it is just once. The exposure changes narratives and shifts perspectives. You become exposed to possibilities, so your worldview becomes broader. Sadly, many of our close relatives do not have a broad enough worldview, so sometimes, their advice and words of wisdom can be limiting. On the flip side, there are some who might not necessarily have a wide worldview but push you to do better and explore possibilities simply because they did not have these opportunities. The point though is that you will be bombarded with many worldviews and even limiting beliefs, but you have to remember that there are no limits, not even the sky.

Embrace uncertainties, struggles, and disappointments as you go after those goals and dreams. What doesn't kill you makes you stronger. The hotter the battle, the sweeter the victory. People might change but the goal does not. Find new people if you must, but don't give up on the dream.

## POWER STEPS

1. Take a moment to write down ten of your limiting beliefs. Then write down the opposite of those limiting beliefs.

2. Recite the positive beliefs every day for at least a month. Don't stop until you believe it. When in doubt, do it all over again.

3. Change your vocabulary. Add words like "yet" to the end of your sentences to create room for possibilities. For example, say, *"I'm not a millionaire yet"* instead of just saying *"I'm not a millionaire."* Adding this three-letter word significantly changes the meaning of the sentence.

4. Be mindful of how you speak. Correct yourself if you must because death and life is in the power of the tongue. Speak positively to yourself.

**Theme Song: "Reach" (Gloria Estefan)**

# *Rule # 9*

## *Do It For Love, Not For Likes*

*"The time spent in trying to impress others could be spent in doing the things by which others would be impressed."*
*—Frank Pierson*

There is a specific scripture that I often remind myself of when I need to do something and feel discouraged.

> *"And whatsoever ye do, do it heartily, as to the Lord, and not unto men." (Colossians 3:23 – KJV).*

I love this scripture because it reminds me of why I should be doing whatever I am doing in the first place. I am doing it unto God, not unto man. My aim should be to impress God, not man. This gives me motivation.

In addition to doing what you do unto God, do it because you love it and not merely to impress others. In other words, do it for love and not for likes. In this social media age, I must admit, this is easier said than done. Everything seems to be about clicks and likes, leaving us to feel lonely and rejected when we do not get enough clicks and likes on our latest posts. For full transparency, even I sometimes fall victim to this and must quickly pull myself out of the pit. The feeling gets even worse when you look at the insights and notice that the post reached hundreds of accounts but only a few people even bothered to like it. Trust me, my friend, you are not alone.

The recipe for this though is simply a different outlook and requires us to redefine our why. Are you doing that thing to impress others or is there a much bigger purpose? I pray your aim will never be to merely impress others or just to receive their compliments. One of the major life lessons I learnt in my teens is to never aim to impress people. I came across a quote that really put things into perspective. According to the quote, *"If you live by people's compliments, you'll die by their criticisms."* This is profound! Having experienced this firsthand, I know for a fact that this is true.

Never get caught up in people's praises. Appreciate and accept compliments and commendations, but never build your self-worth on them. The fact is, human nature is unpredictable. One minute people might be with you but switch teams the moment you are no longer favourable. This is not a lesson on human nature, but this is something worth noting. Let your aim be to not impress man. If you do intend to impress anyone, let it be God. After all, He's worth trying to impress anyway.

Furthermore, aim to do what you love so you don't have to crave others liking it. I started YouTube in February of 2024 after a little encouragement from my coach and, honestly, it has been one of the best decisions I could have made because I really love what I do. I love sitting in front of the camera and motivating, uplifting, and inspiring others. But even amidst this love for what I am doing, I occasionally have to remind myself to do it for the love and not for the likes. I mean, if one life is impacted and I have little to no likes or views, that should be good enough. I would have made a difference in the world while doing what I love.

So, what is that thing for you? What do you actually love to do? It might not be getting enough likes or recognition, but you actually love to do it. Take a moment to think about it. Now that you have thought about at least one thing, my question is, *"What is stopping you from pursuing it?"* Is it your fear of not getting enough likes? Is it your fear of it not being "impressive" enough? By now you should know that those questions have no merit here. Do that thing anyway.

Steve Jobs, co-founder of Apple, was passionate about technology from an early age. This love for technology led to Apple, which is today one of the most successful companies on earth. People are fascinated by iPhones, iPads, and other Apple electronics. We scramble to get the latest iPhone, but what if Steve Jobs had not followed his passion and instead stuck to societal expectations of him? Perhaps we would not have had Apple today and definitely not iPhones.

So, you see, pursuing your passion is key to success. They say do what you love, and you will never work a day in your life. This is a debatable statement, but it definitely has some truth to it. Pursue your passion and it will make what you do more enjoyable and meaningful. Furthermore, your passion is a compass to your purpose. Simply put, your purpose is that thing you were placed on the earth to do. It is that thing you were made for. You know it because you are drawn to it. For example, having worked with youth over the years, whether at church as a youth Sunday School teacher or just volunteering, I now believe that my purpose is aligned with youth development. Had I not pursued my passion, I would not have been writing this book and speaking to you. So, I'm thankful I did, and you should be too.

You will not necessarily figure out your purpose in one day, a month, or even a year. I encourage you to be patient with yourself. Take some time to date yourself and discover your passion. When you find that thing, pursue it. It took me some time to realise that my passion and, thus, my purpose is youth development. This is after years of being drawn to youth and being passionate about their upliftment. So, give yourself grace. This is a marathon, not a sprint. It is a journey and not merely a destination.

## POWER STEPS

1. Take some time to reflect on your passion. What do you really love doing that will make a positive difference in the world? That thing could be the compass to your purpose.

2. Identify your WHY. Why are you even doing that thing in the first place? Is it to get the likes and compliments of 100 people whose life is not changed by what you are doing or to reach at least one person whose life is changed forever? Take some time to think about your WHY. Write it down.

3. Just do it. This is not about perfection. You'll figure it out as you go, but you won't if you don't start.

**Theme Song: "Likes" (Chronixx)**

# Rule # 10

## Challenge Yourself

*"You're not meant to do what is easy. You're meant to challenge yourself."*
*—Justin Timberlake*

One of the most life-changing lessons I have learnt—and continue to learn—is the importance of challenges in our personal development as humans. I know, it might sound ironic, but it is the challenges that actually build us. Or is it really ironic though? Because it is resistance at the gym that builds muscles. Trust me, I know. As someone who has been in the gym consistently for over a year now at the time of writing this book, I can really attest to this fact. In the process, I have had a sprained wrist that took months to heal, but the good news is that I am seeing improvements in my physique. So, a little challenge, like the weights I lift at the gym, builds character and builds your spirit. With that being said, learn to challenge yourself a little. This is how you grow.

I have grown comfortable speaking on many stages over the years. I mentioned that I have spoken at civic events as youth mayor for my parish, have preached in church on several occasions, spoken in front of the prime minister of Jamaica, Andrew Holness, and other elected officials, had a few television interviews, and spoken in front of large audiences as a student. Despite all this experience and exposure, I still get a little nervous before I go on stage, as I have mentioned before. In those moments, I often remind myself that I have done this many times, so this time won't be different. What is often more steadying for me is saying to myself, *"Feel the fear and do it anyway."* Read that again because it is powerful. Yes, feel the fear and do it anyway.

You see, that fear is good, depending on how you view it. First of all, that fear indicates that you are leaving your comfort zone, which is awesome. Secondly, that fear is an indication that you are about to grow. There is good fear and bad fear. Good fear acts as a motivator and protector, pushing you to prepare, improve, and make good decisions. For example, you fear failing your exams, so you study. Or you fear disappointing your parents and your future self, so you stay away from gangs. Bad fear, on the other hand, is that limiting fear. It is the type of fear that holds you back from achieving your goals and taking action. For example, you fear starting a business because you think it might not be a success. But what if it actually becomes a success? Bad fear prevents you from even thinking it could actually be a success.

We encounter good fear and bad fear daily. As I write this book, I encountered them both. Bad fear would have me doubt the potential success, but good fear reminds me that I am doing something new outside my comfort zone and that if one life is impacted, that is good enough. It is all about which one you feed. Do you feed the good or bad? This is why being your own CEO (chief encouragement officer) is important because bad fear will try to visit when you are alone or late at night. You won't always be able to call someone to convince you that things will work out. In those moments, you must take control and remind yourself that things will be okay despite how you might feel in that moment. So, develop a habit of speaking positively to yourself.

Challenging yourself leads to overall growth and development. In my third year of university, I first decided to add a French course to my workload because this move presented an opportunity for me to grow intellectually. Secondly, Canada is a bilingual country, so if I decide to stay in Canada after graduation, I will be more equipped to interact in English and French and be more marketable. Needless to say, the process was definitely not easy. From being asked a question in French and responding in Spanish to struggling with on-the-spot responses at times, the course definitely came with its challenges. I have seen students drop the course, but I made a decision that that was not an option for me. Honestly, I could not wait for what felt like torture at times to end. But guess what? Even in the agony, I was growing in the process. As I write this book, I now speak "un peu" (a little) French and can read and understand it as well. In other words, I am way better than I was when I started. That is the thing about the process: it doesn't feel good at the moment, but the result is worth it. The Bible puts it this way, *"No discipline seems pleasant at the time, but painful. Later on, however, it produces a harvest of righteousness and peace for those who have been trained by it." (Hebrews 12:11 - NIV).*

Know too that you are your own competition. You are running a race against yourself: the yesterday version. That is exactly how I view this book on my journey to positively impact millions of lives. This is a race against myself, and the prize is fulfilling my purpose. I am pursuing my purpose, even when the journey and race get uncomfortable.

Another reason why I am not competing with anyone else is because what is mine cannot—and will not—be for anyone else. It might require hard work, but if it's mine, it's just mine, and no one can have what is mine. In Jamaica, we would say it like this: *"Wah is fi yuh cyaa be unfi yuh."*

With that being said, do not be afraid to challenge yourself. Your growth lies in that challenge.

## POWER STEPS

1. Feel the fear and do it anyway. Yes, that is how you grow. Trust me; you will be glad you took action and become more confident the next time. Make taking action amidst your fears a habit.

2. Identify and limit your bad fears. Instead, empower your good fears.

3. Create a record of at least eight times you overcame bad fear and leaned into your good fear instead. I want you to reflect on these. You will see that taking action and overcoming those bad fears is nothing new. You have been doing this all your life.

**Theme Song: "You Can Get It If You Really Want" (Jimmy Cliff)**

# Rule # 11

## Embrace The Whole of You

*"Be happy with being you. Love your flaws. Own your quirks. And know that you are just as perfect as anyone else, exactly as you are."*
*—Ariana Grande*

I once heard a speaker make a statement about transitioning from one city to another, which I found really inspiring. In speaking about moving from one city to another, the speaker said that he soon found out that *"this is not that."* Yes, that is the prolific line I'm referring to: *"this is not that."* I believe this line also sums up my move from Jamaica to study in Canada. Soon, you find out that this new thing is not that old thing. One place can be totally different from the other, requiring you to adapt.

Canada revealed insecurities I didn't even know I had. From being insecure about my accent to further amplifying my insecurities surrounding my acne, Canada was really revealing. On my journey to embracing my full identity, I am discovering that we all have insecurities, or at least a few things we don't like about ourselves. If you don't, I am going to go ahead and assume you are not human. So, let's hope you can at least relate to what I am saying.

Especially with the increased prominence of social media, I think our insecurities are amplified, even if we don't always notice it. We suddenly start to compare ourselves to others and find faults with ourselves that we didn't even know existed. You suddenly start noticing the pimples on your face, your height, weight, the way you sound and dress, and a list of many other things that seem to be going wrong. Sounds familiar? According to the World Health Organization (WHO), 1 in 7 youth ages 10-19 years old experiences a mental disorder. With the prominence of social media and the onset of the COVID-19 pandemic, this has become an even bigger problem. This is a real global concern.

I don't raise this argument to suggest that social media is bad and that you should quit using it. I only raised it to show how easily our insecurities can rise to the surface and try to define us. For some of us, the insecurities are even more pronounced outside of social media. We sometimes become insecure about the family we came from, the circumstances we grew up in, and our lack, not realizing that those things can be our superpower if we insist on making them so. Let's say you grew up poor or in the middle class; you have an advantage even if you don't notice it. You get to be first: the first to go to university, perhaps, or the first to become financially independent and uplift your family's economic status. Don't underestimate the power of being one of the first to do anything. You get to set the trend for those in your family and the wider community. But you won't be able to do all this and effect change if you don't first see your circumstances as your superpower.

It dawned on me over the summer of 2024 that I am what is considered a first-generation university student. This means I am the child of parents who did not attend university. I realized all this when I was asked to sit on a panel of the same name. I am the first, and that is not only a great milestone but also a powerful one. So, having received the panel questions in advance, there was one question I really thought about: *"What does it mean to be a first-generation student?"* I told the audience that I was from rural St. Thomas in Jamaica and that my studying in Canada signaled what was possible for others in my community. I further went on to say that being the first of anything comes with a certain responsibility, and I believe I am responsible for pulling others up. This is something I really do believe.

There is power in embracing the whole of us. It makes us comfortable in our own skin and gives other people permission to be confident in theirs as well. Even being privileged is also a story, and it might even have its own burden because things are not always as glamorous as they might seem. Also, embrace your mistakes. You might not have wanted things to turn out the way they did, but that is now a part of your story. Never forget you are the one with the pen. You get to change the plot at any time.

Don't dwell on the past. Instead, secure your future. The disciple, Paul, says it like this in Philippians 3:13, *"No, dear brothers and sisters, I have not achieved it, but I focus on this one thing: Forgetting the past and looking forward to what lies ahead." (NLT).* Like Paul, let us look ahead because the best is yet to come.

Long after the COVID-19 pandemic had cooled down, I wore my mask because I was afraid of being judged about my acne. I remember attending a session where I was to introduce myself to the group. After briefly introducing myself, I was asked if I wanted to pull down my mask so that the others could *"see my face."* My immediate and firm response was simply *"No,"* perhaps to the shock of those in the room. No explanation, just one word, *"No."* The truth is, I was not being disrespectful; I was uncomfortable showing my acne-prone face at that moment. But it was this exact moment that became the turning point for me. I went home and dated myself, and the next week, I arrived on campus with no mask and a big smile. You see, I got in touch with myself and realized that I was the only one who really knew my journey with acne and, thus, the only one in a position to judge. The truth is, I have made significant progress over the past few years. Additionally, I have done my part to treat it and continue to do so. Mind you, whether or not I was actually being judged is not the point. The point is that I had to overcome my own mental hurdles. You see, we never fully become whole. There is always something to improve, but never forget how far you have come. Learn to celebrate your wins, no matter how small they might seem. A win is a win.

So, embrace every part of you, the good and the bad. There is power in acceptance. Accept what you have no control over and can't change. Your acceptance could give others permission to do the same.

## POWER STEPS

1. Ask yourself: *"What are my insecurities, and what is behind them?"* I'm going to predict that it is likely the perceived opinions of others. If so, ask yourself, *"Why am I giving people power over my identity and existence?"* Sit with that question for a moment.

2. Take back your power. This might take some time but slow progress is still progress. Start by writing down and reciting positive affirmations about yourself daily. Look at yourself in the mirror and remind YOU of how amazing YOU are. Do this until it becomes a part of your new identity and existence.

3. Document the journey. I want you to start journaling about the progress you are making. You can do this

digitally or in a physical book. In a few years, you will be able to look back and be amazed at how far you have come.

**Theme Song: "I Can See Clearly Now" (Jimmy Cliff)**

# Rule # 12

## Leverage Underestimation

*"Do not underestimate the 'power of underestimation.' They can't stop you, if they don't see you coming."*
*—Unknown*

One of my favourite Biblical stories is that of David and Goliath, the big giant and the little boy. David, a shepherd boy, defeated the giant, Goliath, in a single combat. Who would have thought this possible? Certainly not the onlookers and definitely not Goliath. But this story has a much deeper meaning. Being underestimated can be a good thing. Though David was just a small kid compared to a big giant, what Goliath did not know was that while David would tend the sheep, he would encounter bears and lions that he had to fight and, in those moments, was being prepared for the greatest fight of his life, even if he did not know it at the time.

In life, you will face giants, and sometimes you will even be underestimated, but these are both opportunities, depending on how you view them. I know that being overlooked and undermined can be discouraging, but when people don't expect much from you in the first place, they won't expect you to surpass their expectations. This is the opportunity I was talking about. Work on yourself and defeat that Goliath of low expectation, not to prove your capabilities to them but to yourself because you are your only competition, and the prize is your best version of yourself.

Consider my father, who was underestimated when he went to a coffee farm in St. Andrew, Jamaica, to pick coffee. Yes, at this point he had lost his hand. He told me how impressed and surprised the supervisor was when he saw his bag compared to the other fully-abled people who were also picking coffee. But this is my father for you; always defying the limiting expectations. Or that time when he was playing soccer and overheard a group of people jeering him and questioning his capabilities but who were quickly silenced when he scored a goal for his team. Again, I have personally seen my father defy expectations, so I wasn't even surprised when my cousin, Roxanne, video-called me very excited one day while I was at home in Canada to tell me that my father had just scored a goal at the community football tournament they were at. "No surprise there", I thought. According to my father, deep down, throughout his life, he was always on a mission to defy expectations because of his disability.

Defying expectations is fun! The victory feels sweeter when you know you were underestimated. Just look at Colonel Harland Sanders, who founded Kentucky Fried Chicken (KFC) in his 60s and whose recipe was rejected over 1000 times. Today, KFC is one of the most well-known and successful franchises worldwide. Colonel Sanders was underestimated and even doubted, but it was all worth it.

Don't be discouraged when you are underestimated because of how you look, dress, where you are from, or even how you sound. You could change all these and still remain underestimated. You can't control people's perception of you, and you should never try to. You were not placed on the earth to be a people pleaser, so don't be one of those people.

Being a youth also comes with its own burden. Not only are we sometimes doubted but immensely underestimated. However, youth are creative and intelligent and should be respected and appreciated. We bring new perspectives and ideas to the table that older generations might not have thought about. Youth should also find strength in this and use their voice to represent their views. Youth deserve a seat at the table.

There are, in fact, youth who are demanding a seat at the table. For example, Greta Thunberg, a Swedish environmental activist known for challenging world leaders to do better in mitigating climate change. In 2018, at age fifteen, Thunberg held the first "School Strike for Climate" outside the Swedish parliament, which saw students skipping classes to participate in demonstrations demanding action on climate change from political leaders. She has also spoken at the UN Climate Action Summit, demanding similar change. In 2019, she became the youngest-ever Time Person of the Year, a testament to her far-reaching impact.

As I close this chapter, I believe it is important that I make an appeal to young men. Traditionally, females outperform males, especially academically. Females tend to graduate from college at higher rates and with higher GPAs. When young men drop out of school without the relevant skills for employment, this leaves many young men to the streets and gangs. Let this not be you. Choose not to be another negative statistic. You have what it takes to be the change you want to see. You might be underestimated in your schools, community, and even the wider society, but that is your superpower. You have the power within to change the narrative by becoming the best version of yourself and a value to society. Make your family, the world, and especially yourself proud.

Make being underestimated your strength and not a hindrance to your success. You got this! Others have succeeded despite being underestimated, and you can too.

## POWER STEPS

1. Lean into your support system. Don't forget that there are people in your corner who actually love and respect you. These are the people who matter in your success anyway, not those underestimating.

2. Lean into that thing deep down inside you that tells you that you are destined for more. You know what I am talking about. It is that thing that has led you to this book. Lean into it and continue working on fulfilling your purpose and becoming the best version of yourself. Don't be distracted.

3. Remain kind. Don't let being overlooked and undermined turn you into someone you are not. You only have control over yourself and your response. Your time of victory will come.

**Theme Song: "Turning Around For Me" (VaShawn Mitchell)**

# Rule # 13

# Pick Yourself Up

*"Just because you make a mistake doesn't mean you are a mistake."*
*—Georgette Mosbacher*

At my church back in Jamaica, we would sing a song that goes something like this, *"If you stumble and fall, my brother, if you stumble and fall, my friend, pick yourself up and turn yourself around, and start all over again."* This is a song that speaks volumes about life. You will make mistakes and sometimes mess up along the journey, but that is a part of the journey. When you mess up, find the courage to pick yourself up. I know the song says to pick yourself up and start all over again, but in reality, you are not starting all over; this time, you are starting from experience.

I know I have told you a lot about my successes, but trust me, I have had those failures too. I have stumbled and fallen many times. After all, I am only human like you. I have often done things or acted out of selfish desires, whether against God or my fellow brothers and sisters. Yes, I have had to ask for forgiveness from both God and people. I have had to forgive myself. Yes, you heard me right! I have had to forgive myself.

This is another major aspect of picking one's self up after stumbling and falling. Sometimes we are so hard on ourselves—especially those over-achievers like myself. We become so accustomed to getting it right and being admired that we sometimes forget that we too are human.

I will never forget one birthday in high school when I started getting a flood of messages telling me how much of a role model I was, how much I was loved and admired, and how overwhelmed I felt. I know these are all great messages, but they overwhelmed me. The messages brought my flaws before my eyes, and I started to feel like a fraud, a failure even. But since then, I have learnt the importance of giving myself grace.

Our desire to be perfect can be crippling and can hinder our greatness. First of all, God doesn't even call us to be perfect. We strive for perfection largely because of how we think others will accept us. I say aim to make progress and not to be perfect. You might ruin your life and mental health trying to be perfect. It is not worth it!

My friend, you can't do life without a few stumbles and falls. That is a part of the journey, as I have told you many times. Life is not a paved highway with no potholes. No, life is more like a pothole-covered road heading into a rural community like mine. You might manage to escape a few potholes, but I am sure you will end up falling into at least one of them. But do you park your car and decide not to continue the journey? No, you don't. You move ahead more cautiously as you head to your destination. So, do the same when you face a few of life's potholes because, trust me, you will. Your stumbles and falls aren't life sentences, so don't make them out to be.

When you pick yourself up, pick up those lessons that come along with the journey too, because picking yourself up will give others permission to do the same. You never know who might be watching and gaining courage from your courage. Messing up does not have to be final unless you make it final. Have you had a child in your teens? Pick yourself up. Got drawn into gangs? Pick yourself up. Have you started to undervalue yourself? Pick yourself up. Whatever the case, you have the power in you to shift course. It might take some time, but remember, the aim is progress, not perfection.

Just imagine if Sarah Jakes Roberts, the well-known pastor and author, had not picked herself up after becoming pregnant at thirteen and having her son at fourteen while her father, Bishop TD Jakes, was a well-known bishop in the United States and around the world. It definitely wasn't easy, as Sarah often reminds her congregation. The experience, for her, was shameful, and she felt judged, perhaps because she felt as though she had let down herself and her family. Unfortunately, many teens who become pregnant see their pregnancy as a life sentence, but it is not. The reality is that they have the power within to pick themselves up.

You might need a little support along the way. This is where your support system comes in handy. But even if you don't have a solid support system at the moment, there are a few trusted people you can speak to, such as guidance counselors, a pastor or an equivalent, teachers, and others. Seek out one or a few trusted people. You are not in this alone.

There is no shame in not having it together. In fact, it is okay not to be okay. There is strength in even knowing you need help in the first place. This takes being in touch with oneself, and not many are in touch with themselves, so celebrate the fact that you can identify when you need help.

Thomas Edison, the inventor of the light bulb, failed over a thousand times while trying to invent the light bulb. What if he had given up after the third or even the one-hundredth failure? Perhaps the people of his time would not have been blessed by this new invention, and perhaps we wouldn't have been either. Edison is credited with saying: *"I have not failed. I've just found 10,000 ways that won't work."* Again, it is all about how you view things. See failure as an opportunity to be better and to do better.

## POWER STEPS

1. Actively work on changing your perspective on life and your stumbles. Ask yourself, *"How can I grow from this? What lessons are there to learn?"*

2. Make a decision to actually learn the lessons from these mistakes. This time, you should be wiser so act wiser and be wiser.

3. If you stumble and fall again, pick yourself up again.

**Theme Song: "Ain't No Giving In" (Chronixx)**

# Rule # 14

# Do Not Be Burdened By The Weight of Expectations

*"Trying to maintain everyone else's standards for my life is unsustainable."*
*—Johanna Schram*

In one of my Social Studies classes in high school, I was introduced to the "looking-glass self" theory, which I found really eye-opening. According to this theory developed by American sociologist, Charles Horton Cooley, the "looking-glass self" is where people base their identity on how they believe people see them. We use our social interactions as a type of "mirror," so we use the judgments of others to measure our own worth, value, and behaviour. There are stages to the "looking-glass self." Firstly, an individual imagines how they appear to others in a social interaction. Secondly, the individual imagines the judgment of others. And lastly, the individual develops feelings about those judgments and responds to them.

We often say things like, *"I don't care what anyone thinks."* But most, if not all the time, this is not the truth. We do care what others think. We take a bath and put on deodorant. Why? Because we do care what others think. We gct our hair done and iron our clothes. Why? Because we do care what others think. I believe what we really mean when we say we don't care what others think is that we don't care to the point where people's opinion of us bothers us. Sadly, it sometimes does. Trust me, I can relate, but based on my own observation, you will become less bothered by age and experience. So, this too is a process.

With the advent of social media comes the weight of expectation. We scroll through Instagram, Twitter, Snapchat, and TikTok and believe what we see is what is expected of us. So, we buy the things we can't afford to impress people we don't even know. I felt like I had won an Olympic gold medal in October of 2023 when I was in Jamaica for a week, and a friend made a comment about my phone. He was shocked to notice that I still had the same old Samsung Galaxy phone I had years before while I was living in Jamaica. To me, that was such a huge compliment. Let's just say I prioritize things other than the latest iPhone. Let me also add that I have nothing against iPhones. I am merely making a point.

Remember earlier I told you to invest in your future today? I would rather invest in myself and my future than buy things just to impress people or simply because they are in style. Don't forget that styles and trends change, so you will have to purchase again just to keep up. This desire to keep up can be expensive, draining and, frankly, unnecessary. If you decide to follow suit, do it because you can afford to and or want to. Don't do it simply because society expects you to.

Have you ever noticed how some well-known millionaires and billionaires dress? Sometimes the way they dress could be considered underwhelming, but guess what? They have nothing to prove to anyone and have no one to impress, especially not broke people. This is why it is possible that we are passing actual millionaires on a daily basis simply because they don't dress the way we think they should, drive the cars we think they should, or live in the house we think they should. This was one of the key lessons I learnt from the very popular book, "The Millionaire Next Door: The Surprising Secrets of America's Wealthy" by Thomas J. Stanley. *"Don't judge a book by its cover,"* as they say.

We spoke about being underestimated, and sadly, you too might be judged because of how you look and dress and even by your latest technological devices or lack thereof. But you are too young to be caught up! I urge you to spend time working on improving yourself and positioning yourself for success instead of trying to live up to people's expectations and put on a show. Do the work today so you can reap the reward tomorrow.

We will even feel the weight of expectations from close friends and family. This can be a bit more complicated because these are the people in our support system. This might require you to have some tough but important conversations. You shouldn't be expected to become a doctor simply because your parents are doctors. You should be given the freedom to walk your own path. After all, this is your journey and not that of others. If you are experiencing any of this, take some time to have a conversation with your parents or loved ones. Just imagine if Usain Bolt, the fastest man in the world, was discouraged from athletics simply because his parents felt that that was not a traditional path and forced him into another profession. Maybe the world would not have been blessed by his talent and his name so recognizable today. So, walk your own path and follow your passion. I have a feeling it will lead to a beautiful destination.

Giving in to expectations will only leave you bankrupt, especially when what is expected of you is not in line with your life's purpose.

## POWER STEPS

1. Again, get in touch with your passion, and when you do, pursue it.

2. Make a decision every day not to be defined by people's expectations. Emphasis on the word "decision."

3. If loved ones are shoving their expectations at you, have a sit-down conversation with them. It is better to pursue your passion than the passion of others.

**Theme Song: "Three Little Birds" (Bob Marley)**

# *Rule # 15*

# *Don't Let The Tough Times Fool You*

*"Show me someone who has done something worthwhile, and I'll show you someone who has overcome adversity."*
*—Lou Holtz*

"*This too shall pass*" is a line I heard my grandmother use many times, and as a result, it is a line I have grown to adapt. It reassures me that despite the tough times and challenges I might face, better and brighter days are ahead. Knowing my grandmother's life story means knowing the power of those four simple words.

When I was about three years old, my grandmother lost her daughter, my mother, suddenly, and before the year had ended, her son, my uncle, also died, leaving my grandmother to grapple with the death of her two children and the future of her two grandchildren, myself and my cousin. So, now you know the power and meaning behind those four words, *"this too shall pass."* Her own struggles and loss gave her credibility to give others that advice. She has faced her own challenges and survived.

Sorry, I didn't mean to cause doom and gloom. Lighten up! I am merely making a point about perseverance. We will all face tough times, but the good news is that they don't last. They might feel permanent at the moment, but this is not the truth.

During the height of the COVID-19 pandemic, one of my friends taught me the concept of the *"illusion of permanency."* He reminded me that though tough times might feel permanent, this is only an illusion. So, as you grow and face challenges—because you will—I want you to remember this concept my friend taught me and remind yourself that the perception that tough times won't end is only an illusion. I have personally faced challenges that I thought would never end, but they did.

Just look at Joseph, the young boy from the Bible who was thrown into a pit by his jealous brothers, sold into slavery, lied on, and then thrown into prison after finally starting to climb the social ladder. But guess what? He would go on to become the prime minister of Egypt. I can only imagine how discouraging all this might have been, but the tough times didn't last. This is definitely a story of resilience. The story can be found from Genesis 37 to Genesis 50 in the Bible and is among my favourites. I love a triumphant story! Like Joseph, choose to be better and not bitter.

Then there is the story of another biblical character named Job, a very wealthy and god-fearing man who would later lose all his possessions, including his ten children, in a very short time. But guess what? He would later recover everything and receive twice as much as he had. He was also blessed with a long life and ten more children, including three daughters, who were the most beautiful women in all the land. The story of Job can be found in the book of Job in the Bible. God has a way of creating beauty out of ashes. Romans 8:28 puts it like this, *"And we know that all things work together for good to them that love God, to them who are the called according to his purpose." (KJV).* This is a significant reassurance because it shows us that the good things will work in our favour and even the bad things. You should be thrilled to hear this.

I once heard a speaker tell an audience to be mindful of two Ds in life: discouragement and distractions. This makes so much sense because these are two things that will really come at us as we seek to progress. Things will happen to make you feel discouraged, and things will happen that will seek to distract you. The fact is that life will have challenges, but nothing lasts forever, especially the tough times.

Do you remember the COVID-19 pandemic and the lockdowns that came with it? Do you remember how, in those moments, it all seemed like this would never end and the world would not go back to "normal"? But things got better, right? As I write this book, masks are no longer mandatory, and we are definitely not under a lockdown. The simple truth is that things get better over time.

I know that as a youth, at our age, challenges might sometimes seem bigger than they are. When you face those tough times, just remind yourself, *"this too shall pass."*

## POWER STEPS

1. When you face tough times, take a moment to reflect on the challenges you have overcome in the past. As you will see, you have overcome many challenges in the past, so the current challenges won't be any different.

2. Speak positively to yourself and lean into your support system.

3. Believe that you have all it takes in you to overcome because you really do. You got this!

**Theme Song: "Better Days" (Le'Andria Johnson)**

# Rule # 16

## Don't Wait To Be Great

*"If you are searching for greatness, then check yourself. Greatness is in you. You just need to unearth it."*
*—Damor McQueen*

For a moment, I want you to pause and think about your many dreams and goals— the house, cars, career, and even becoming wealthy. Just imagine how quickly those might become a reality if you take small steps today instead of waiting for tomorrow. Live like you don't have time. No, I am not telling you to go partying, get drunk, and forget all you did the night before. I know that when you are told to live like you don't have time, that is usually what you are being encouraged to do. But not today. I am instead telling you to take action. I am sure you have some big dreams. Don't you? If I were to ask you, *"Where do you see yourself in the next 10-15 years?"* what would be your response? Pause and think about this question as well.

Maybe you thought about owning a huge mansion, a BMW, a multimillion-dollar company, being at the top of your profession, or even owning a few businesses. Whatever those dreams are, what are you currently doing to make them a reality? Or were you waiting on greatness instead of pursuing it right now? I would hope not. Don't wait to be great!

Take steps today to ensure that your many goals and aspirations become a reality. What if I were to ask you about the top five celebrities you most admire? You might mention artists such as Beyonce and Justin Bieber, actors such as Kevin Hart and Dwayne "the Rock" Johnson, billionaires such as Oprah Winfrey and Tyler Perry, athletes such as Shelly-ann Fraser-Pryce and Usain Bolt, and the list continues. These are all notable individuals who are known around the world. However, they didn't suddenly just become great one day. Their greatness was nurtured. They were all once in obscurity with no notoriety. However, with work, consistency, and determination, they are known and recognized worldwide today.

What if you were to start honing your skills early and working on those big dreams you have starting today? Can you imagine where you might end up in a few years? I have personally envisioned this, and that is exactly why I am not waiting for greatness. I have decided to use the tools from this book, including my support system and self-determination, to propel myself ahead. I am not waiting for greatness to find me. I am going to go looking for it.

Never forget that greatness starts small. So, pursuing greatness for you could be volunteering at school or in your local community, as I have done in the past. By giving of your time, you are learning to be selfless and the importance of service, which are all important on your path to greatness. So, despise not the day of small beginnings. Get involved. Do the work now. Don't wait to be great.

I find that the enemy of action for many young people is the belief that we have all the time in the world, but do you really think so? Time moves by very quickly while you are delayed in taking action. The days, months, and years are moving by really quickly. Remember, time waits on no man.

Starting early also means you get to fail early, which is good. While you are failing, you are also figuring out how to succeed. This is an opportunity in itself. Imagine starting a business in your teens. Can you imagine where that business could be five or ten years down the line? It could literally be the next big thing. But you won't know until you actually start.

Now that I think about it, unknowingly, my involvements, leadership roles, etc., were all part of a journey toward greatness. It was simply me not waiting to be great. I am definitely not saying I am great right now, but I am definitely making progress. Also, I think greatness is subjective and very personal. What I might consider great, you might not consider great. So, I would advise you to work on being the best version of yourself. I think that that qualifies as greatness.

I am also not waiting to be great by writing this book. My advice is being put into action as I write this book. Who knows what this book might become? I certainly don't, but it could be the next big thing. I guess we will just have to wait and see. Try early. Fail early. Succeed early. Take risks and do big things in small ways now. Just look at Marley Dias, who, at the young age of eleven in 2015, started the #1000blackgirlbooks social media campaign in an effort to collect and donate 1000 books featuring black girls as the main characters. She has far surpassed her original target. Her campaign brought to the attention of people the limited representation of women of colour as main characters in books. She is the author of "Marley Dias Gets it Done and So Can You," and in 2018, she was featured as the youngest member of Forbes' 30 under 30 ever selected.

It would be remiss of me not to also mention my friend, Rajae Lewis, who, at age eighteen, founded the Live Love Laugh Youth Foundation, a non-profit organization in Jamaica that seeks to create opportunities for and uplift children, youth, senior citizens, and the disabled. Rajae's passion for community development has not gone unnoticed; his many awards and recognitions are proof of this. Rajae, like so many other youths in Jamaica and around the world, is proof that youths can do big things.

A good place to start is by setting goals (long and short-term). For the purpose of this book, we will define short-term goals as objectives that can be achieved in a month. So, a short-term goal on your journey to greatness could be for you to review all the power steps in this book within a month and take action as you prepare for your journey to greatness. Let us then define long-term goals as those that can be achieved within a one-year period. A long-term goal could be that within a year of reading this book, you would have implemented the business idea you had in your head but had never taken action on before. Set long and short-term goals to make those big dreams you have a reality. Take action. Remember that time is going by while you might be delaying taking action.

Since the start of this book, I have given you many tools to get you started. Please do not fall victim to analysis paralysis. This is where you over-analyze a situation and then end up not taking action. Don't just consume the information but also execute it. Take action today. Go be great!

## POWER STEPS

1. Reflect on all sixteen rules of this book. Make your own summary of each, along with 1-3 takeaways.

2. If you haven't taken action on the practical steps at the end of each chapter, please return and do so.

3. Again, take action. Reread if you must.

**Theme Song: "Hall of Fame" (The Script)**

# Call to Action

Now that you have read my rules of success, started taking action on the power steps, and received inspiration from the theme songs, I hope you are fueled and ready to walk the path of success and greatness. Remember that this is a journey and not a destination. You will sometimes face challenges, but this is a part of life. These challenges can—and will—position you as a victor if you allow them to. Don't give up when it gets hard. Your brother, Damor, is in your corner. Let us run towards our great future ahead!

As we navigate this journey together, I urge you to stay in touch as there are resources and initiatives to come from this book. Connect with me on Instagram, Facebook, Twitter, YouTube, and my other social media handles at Damor McQueen. Yes, just my first and last name. Let's keep it simple.

I also urge you to post a photo with the book, a line, or chapter that stood out to you using these three hashtags:

#successrulesrewritten, #youthagainstlimits, #youthguide4success.

Thank you for reading.

There are great things ahead for you. See you at the top!

# About the Author

Damor McQueen is a 23-year-old youth leader and catalyst for change who is on a mission to create positive global disruptions and leave a lasting legacy. Having had years of experience as a youth leader and providing mentorship to youth, he believes that his purpose is aligned with youth development, so he strives to help develop and empower the next generation of youth leaders.

In 2017, he founded the youth-led Bumpy Purpose Foundation, which seeks to educate youth and help them unlock their purpose. He is a rural youth from the community of Middleton, in St. Thomas, Jamaica, who is currently studying in Canada. It is successes like these that he seeks to use as a reminder to youth from all walks of life that success is possible, no matter one's upbringing or socio-economic background. Damor seeks to lift as he climbs.

www.ingramcontent.com/pod-product-compliance
Lightning Source LLC
LaVergne TN
LVHW051248080426
835513LV00016B/1811

* 9 7 8 1 9 5 8 4 4 3 9 2 7 *